Pub Lives
in
Poetry

By Tony Smith

To Rose + Chris
Best Wishes

A CIP catalogue record for this title is available from the
British Library.

Published in 2014 by FeedARead Publishing

v.9

A Dedication

The Station Inn has served many roles in my life over the last twenty five years:

It has served as a well, from which I have drawn - a little too often it is said by some. It made my life bearable during difficult times, providing a sanctuary which I shared with a host of people, many of whom became close friends.

It has been a 'bolt hole' to which I could escape in order to offload inconsequential matters, to tell jokes and the 'odd' yarn to people who I knew would listen with sympathy, understanding and good humour.

It has been a refuge, where I could go to lick my wounds following the crises and incidents occasioned by my alcoholic lapses and withdrawals.

Most importantly of all, it has been a place of warmth and camaraderie, where I could experience the well meant jibes and banter, exchange wit and wisdom – and occasionally philosophy - and participate in the community that grew, married, celebrated and marked the passing of some of those around us.

Some years ago, I began to mark these communal occasions with a poem and, with the exception of a few short breaks, have continued ever since with what has become something of a tradition.

It has been a great adventure to share so many good times with this assortment of fun loving, charismatic, sharp witted and amusing friends, some of whom sadly are no longer with us.

This book is dedicated to them and to the community of friends which is The Station Inn.

Tony Smith
April 2014

Index

"To myself – without whose brilliance and genius

I could not have completed this work…"

Pub lives in poetry…

Iron Tits farewell...

I was going to say something clever,
I was going to say something smart.
I was going to say that forever,
You would live in our minds as a tart.

But no, it is time to be truthful,
To say all the things that are true.
To say that, dear Mrs Leslie,
It's true that we all will miss you.

And when you are gone Mrs Leslie,
And when you are just a has been,
We want you to know Mrs Leslie,
You will be forever, our Queen.

Your reign has been one of terror.
A rigid regime, oh so hot.
But your judgement was often in error,
You kept going off, with that Scot.

But believe us when we say, good luck Liz.
Believe us when we say farewell.
Our love and best wishes go with you,
And fond happy memories as well.

Your bollockings, bannings and banter,
Will always remain in our heart.
And a soul that's as good as old Santa,
Is the thing which will set you apart.

1

So here's to you our dear Lizzie,
And here's to your happiness too.
God knows how you're going to keep busy,
When you haven't got us to look to.

Goodbye and good luck and God bless dear,
And we all hope that you will keep well.
And remember the ones that you leave here,
Who all made your life, such a hell.

Chris and Sara's wedding

We have this dear friend, we call Chris'
Who frequently goes on the piss.
And although he gets fatter,
It really don't matter,
Cos the reason we love him is this;

He's a pal he's a mate, he's a mucker,
He's a fool he's a friend, he's a sucker,
And we wouldn't be sorry,
If he drove a lorry,
Cos he'd make a bloody good trucker.

He's clever, he's smart and he's bright,
Sometimes incoherently tight,
And although Liz has banned him,
And we can't understand him,
We think he'll be alright tonight.

But now he has got his comeuppance,
His drinking career is worth tuppence.
No way could it last,
Tis a thing of the past.
And the ciders come down about thruppence.

Though he's had some ups and some downs,
And we've shared some smiles and some frowns.
But the finest thing yet,
Is that Christopher met,
Dear Sara, the best girl in town.

So now they are both man and wife,
And love and good feelings are rife.
Let's see them kiss,
And all wish them this;
Happiness, for the rest of their life.

Chris Webster's 50th - 2002

It's his party today and we can't get away
From the fact that he's fifty at last.
Though many will say, there was never a way,
That they thought that the bugger would last.

I think he'll admit, that he does drink a bit,
And we've all had a spot in our time.
But the worrying thing, is that it makes him sing,
And he dances as well; it's a swine!

I wouldn't like to say, that folks wouldn't pay,
Just to see him and hear him perform.
But I wouldn't do that, he sounds like our cat,
And it looks like his knees are deformed.

He builds things as well, as poor Sara will tell,
His ambition is not such a crime.
But it has to be said, wether kitchen or shed,
That they all take a bloody long time.

The Egyptians were good, but it's well understood,
That this bloke works at such a slow rate.
That if ever he did, build a great pyramid,
Tutankhamen would just have to wait.

His dogs just as bad, the bloody things mad,
He's jet black, and as big as a horse.
One minute he'll paw you, and then he'll ignore you,
His names bloody Webster, of course.

They took him away, on a weeks holiday,
Or it may well have been a fortnight.
I said to Sar-a, did he shit in the car?
She said "yes, but the dog was alright"

4

Chris likes practical jokes, you know, torturing folks,
Shaves his beard, and wears funny clothes.
I've seen him dressed as a tart; he does look the part,
(Oh! I shouldn't have said that. No one knows.)

But now like I say, he's fifty today,
And we're all gathered round him to cheer.
And we'd like to say this; that we all love you Chris.
All those who agree, say Here! Here!
HERE! HERE!!!!!

Descent

Spiral spiral,
Little man,
Down you go into the can,
Slither down the greasy track,
For this time you'll not come back,
Down you go
And all before,
Will not matter anymore.

Michael Antill (7th April 1950 – 19th August 2001)

I tried to think of words that would best describe Mike; 'laid back' certainly came to mind. He had the most wonderful temperament; he treated most of the problems in his life with an unruffled calm. 'Clever' was another, he certainly was clever. He could rattle off a crossword quicker than most of us could say, Brachiopod.
He was also 'talented', with a great ear for music and the ability to play guitar and keyboard well. Many of us will think of him when songs like, 'Take it Easy', 'Under the Boardwalk' and 'Rockabye Sweet Baby James' are played.
'Humorous' - he certainly was humorous. A few days before he died I went to see him. He was watching television, I said "Hello mate, what you watching?" He said "Pissin impossible", and he said that he had just been watching a film about a doctor who had prepared a register for all chicken-pox related illness. I said, "Oh yes, what's it called?" He said, "Shingles List". Then, later, when I quoted some Shakespeare to him he said, "I know that – that's from the Merchant of Bloxwich 'ay it?"
But it was the word 'kind' which eventually came top in my mind.
He was a kind man.
He rarely had a bad word to say about anyone. He couldn't ban anyone from his pub, he would always excuse them, "They're all right", he would say, "They don't mean any harm".
Even Peter was safe.
Yes he was kind. I'm sure that Sue and Vanessa, with whom he shared so many years of his life, will agree with that.
He left us with some nice memories.
He left us with some nice people.
He left us with 'the Bear Club': the charming lively Danni, the sweet natured and pretty Jess, the warm and friendly Lee (so like his father) and the incomparable Joey Bear, the lovely Jo who has been such a wonderful example of strength and love over these last few painful months. God Bless Tye, who was always there for her and Sally, who was so supportive.
Let us comfort ourselves with the memory that although his life was too short, it was a relatively active one.

He wasn't a commercial animal; in fact "Take it Easy" should have been his signature tune.

He loved his life, he loved his family, he loved his music and he loved his golf.

Yes, I am sure that wherever he is now, he'll be playing a round of golf, or if it's raining, he'll be having a drink and doing the crossword. Perhaps we should be a little more like him. Perhaps we should take time to smell the flowers.

Farewell Mike, we loved you, we will miss you, we will remember you.

Ready! Sheddy! Go!

(The Websters shed inauguration
Saturday 3rd November 2001.)

I declare that this shed,
The bestest shed,
It will be said,
When plans are read,
And we're all dead,
That Websters shed,
To give him cred',
And swell his head,
When we've been fed,
This bloody shed,
Is open!

Mark Blakeway's 40th birthday

Please make way for Blakeway, he's 40 years old.
The remarkable thing is that no-one was told.
Although it was whispered and rumours were plenty,
He always told us he was just over twenty.

But now we all know and we're glad to be here,
To eat all his food and to drink all his beer.
And though not to tell us was terribly naughty,
We'll have a good time and forget that he's forty.

But we will not forget he's a bloody good sort,
With his family, his farming, his friends and his sport.
And no doubt we'll find out, he's a bloody good host.
So let's lift up our glasses and give him the toast.

Happy Birthday dear Marcus we all wish you well.
Thank you for this 'Barbie' and Cheryl as well.
Forty summers have come, forty summers have gone.
And we'll be here next year, when there's been forty one.

"Happy Birthday"

My Son Steven and Lindsay - the wedding

Dear Steven and Lindsay we're all gathered here,
To share in your happiness free food and beer,
And to wish you the best in your forthcoming life,
If there will be a best now your both man and wife.

Your prospects are rosy and I hope you will be,
Content: just like what nearly happened to me,
When I saw you today I thought what a nice pair,
And our Stevens ok if he'd just comb his hair.

But I know I am I lucky to be standing here,
It ain't just the free food or even the beer,
I'm lucky because my son's a great bloke,
And still loves his father although he is broke.

I'm lucky because he has shown such good taste,
In choosing dear Lindsay in love not in haste,
And choosing to work and not choosing to waste,
And living and loving and still staying chaste.

I love them like you do and wish them the best,
And know that their love will now pass any test,
So fill up your glasses and let's wish them health,
A life of fulfillment and friendship and wealth.

They are both lovely people who we're lucky to know,
And today we are lucky to see their love grow,
So let's toast them now that's if you can find room,
To Lindsay and Steven: The Bride and the Groom.

Mystery Lady 1

I look at you and I know why you often do avert your eye,
I stare at you and often think that you do know a truth from lie,
I share with you the great contempt with people that we have to know,
And I could drink your deep brown eyes but that I know I know you
know.

And I so love your elegance your oval face your lovely form,
Your everything I love in life your slender lithe and ever warm,
And like I said if I could be a castaway on some far shore,
I know that I would come to love you more and more and more.

So lovely lady come my way and dally with me for one day,
And let me kiss your red warm lips and sip with you my gentle sips,
And for that one quiet lovely time but for one hour be mine be mine,
And though the rest will be regret we will be happy that we met.

Sara's 50th

Sara Patricia. The occasion today,
Will allow me to say what we'd all like to say,
Your decision to marry Chris Webster was Quaint,
For most normal women would think you're a saint.

I love you we love you and always we will,
Not as much as old Webster who thinks you're a thrill,
You are warm and sincere and consistently kind,
But you still married Webster you must have been blind.

I know that you loved him and married in haste,
And there's like they say, no accounting for taste,
But now you are fifty and you've made your bed,
And you must lie on it, but it must be said.

You're our greatest hostess, your parties are great,
You make us feel welcome, your food is first rate,
And as nice people go you would pass any test,
For Sara Patricia, you're 'Simply the best'.

Mike Dalzell - deceased

I knew Mike for most of his life.
We were five year olds, together at Foley Park Infants School.
And through junior school, Sladen Secondary Modern,
And on to Kiddeminster College of Further Education.
We lost touch a little throughout the 70s,
But over recent years reconnected and again became firm friends.

He was a success of course and it was a private joke between us,
When I often said to him, "Of course we both started with nothing,
And I went slowly downhill!"

We did some business together and he always grumbled in a good
Natured way about what he called my extortionate charges
But he always paid promptly and with a flourish.

He also had that very rare quality, of the ability to laugh at himself.
We teased him unmercifully about the length of time it took for the
Penny to drop when he heard funny story;

Joan told me that he would often start giggling when they were in bed
in the small hours of the morning. And she would say "What's the
matter?"
And he would say I've just got that joke that Topsy told two days ago.

When we were young, the Dalsells were one of the few families who
had a television.
Workhouse boots were more common than T.Vs in those days.
And Mike used to take me home to their house in Clee Avenue to
watch
Robin Hood. It was over 50 years ago.
But I remember.

I remember Mike as a good natured, generous, friendly little boy.
And so he remained until the day he died.
A good natured, generous, friendly little boy.
We loved him, and we will miss him.

14

'Sammy'

Small tough girl,
I saw you cry,
Unnoticed by the standers by.
Small tough girl,
You don't fool me.
You're sensitive and kind,
You see.

You serve your booze,
And strut your stuff,
And think that,
That will be enough.

And shout at us,
And boss us all,
And we like fools,
Obey the call.

Of A! you 'aven't paid for that
And oy! You're drunk.
Get out you twat.

But small tough girl,
You don't fool me,
You're sensitive,
And kind you see.

Nic and Tim – the wedding

For Nic and Tim', t'was very grim,
When they began a'courtin',
He loved her, she hated him,
Which wasn't very sportin'.

Each used to come to me and say,
The other one was "orrid",
But all the time I knew that they,
Had something, which was torrid.

The years went by and gradulii,
Their love grew ever stronger,
And times between the rows they had,
Went on for hours, and longer.

And I have watched this growing bond,
And seen this love match flower,
Observed the way they laugh and love,
And shout and scowl and glower.

The mix of blood will help them build,
A marriage strong as rock,
His Dads a 'Yank', his Mam's a 'Taff',
And he's a 'Sweaty sock'.

And Nic's a good old Kiddy girl,
there's nothing wrong with that,
If I'd been twelve months younger,
Well! We won't go into that.

For my part, oh I wish them well,
And hope they both will be,
As happy as my wife and I,
Thought we were going to be.

And when they came into the room,
We saw a glorious pair,
And Tim looked pretty good as well,
If it wasn't for his hair.

So here we are to see them wed,
And gladly flows my pen,
Some thought it would not happen,
And Steve owes Lizzie ten.

We wish you love and happiness,
And wealth and health and more,
We wish you all you wish yourselves,
And children by the score.

And when this bash is over,
And the leaving car departs,
Take with you these fond memories,
Take with you our fond hearts.

Jo and Tye - wedding, 6th June 2002

When Jo approached me and said "Topsy, I'm getting married"
I was shocked,
I said, I didn't even know you were pregnant.
She said, "Will you give me away?"
I said, "I won't tell a soul".

Anyway I said, "Who's the lucky man",
She said "certainly not you, you fat old bastard",
Well as usual I'd got it all wrong,
So here we are.
And what a lovely sight,
Radiant, lovely hair, glittering eyes, flashing smile,
And I think Jo's made a good effort as well.
I think you will all agree with me,
That they are a lovely couple,
And Tye's got a lot going for him too.

Anyway, I would like to say,
That I consider it a great honor,
That I have been asked to do this today,
And I know that we all will be thinking of,
And remembering the nice bloke,
Who should be stood here.
I know he'll be looking down at us,
Grinning that grin,
And I know that he would know,
That I love his little girl,
Almost as much as he did.

Like all good relationships,
Jo and Tye,
Have had many ups and downs,
Many fall outs, shouting matches,
And squabbles.
Some of them almost equaling,
The onset of World War Three.

18

But such is the mark,
Of all good and enduring relationships,
The rifts were soon healed,
And the partings short lived.
They have come through so much together,
It can only be love.

* * *

And so it falls to me to say,
Please have a happy life,
And Tye, you love Jo every day,
She'll be a smashing wife,
And Jo, you'll always love your man,
I know that's what you're thinking,
So be good to him, I know you can,
And try to stop him drinking.
We wish you love and happiness,
And long and happy years,
Now raise your glasses one and all,
The bride and groom, "Three cheers".

Lisa and Steve's wedding reception - 6th September 2003

All welcome today to see Lisa and Steve,
Celebrate their new union, and we're led to believe,
That this splendid event has, despite all the stress,
Turned a 'heavenly angel' into a 'princess'.

They were meant for each other and it's all very plain,
They'd share a lot more than a wedding dress train,
Little Lisa had toy trains which is pretty rare,
And Steve works for Virgin ... But, let's not go there!

Steve's a Gunners supporter, it's sad but it's true,
And Lisa loves Steve, now she's one fru and fru,
And though Brighton and Rugby are so far apart,
Fate and destiny rule in affairs of the heart.

I am told it was 'dolphin talk' got Steve his wife,
I suppose it gave Lisa some 'porpoise' in life,
They like 'Shakin Stevens' and will possibly more,
Likely get an 'Old House' prob'ly with a 'Green Door'.

In Cyprus it was, when Steve plighted his troth,
Waves crashing on rocks, with the spume and the froth,
The sea was so noisy, the evening, so hot,
 Lisa then turned to Steven, and answered, "You What?"

But it all worked out well and so now we can see,
What a great Bride and Bridegroom they've turned out to be,
So let's charge our glasses, and wish a 'Good Life',
To Steven and Lisa, as husband and wife.

New World Lament - life without alcohol

It was bad today,
Bad for the longest time since our parting,
They say it's like bereavement,
The sense of loss,
The 'something missingness' of it.
Still your fragrance haunts,
But the soothing hand upon my mind is gone,
What times we had you and I,
You protected me from the proper way of things,
From the real pale world I now endure,
You created euphoric ups,
And melancholy downs,
But it was never dull,
As dull as this,
You must not be recalled my dear lost friend,
But what will fill this void but you,
In this New World.

Tyrone's 40th

The toast is; Tyrone, he's one on his own,
And now he is 40 poor sod.
And although he's still here,
He came very near,
To having it all on his tod.

He's crept back in favour, and is now this month's flavour,
But he hasn't done this on the cheap.
What he has done so far,
Is bought Jo, a new car,
It's an Audi T.T...bloody creep!

I heard Jo say once, "He's a bit of a ponce"
I said, I heard that; and don't think it's true.
She then said "Oh dear!
You weren't meant to hear,
I was actually talking about you."

Getting back to our Ty, he's our sort of guy.
He likes loving and kissing and hugs.
He loves his dear wife,
And the good things in life,
Like alcohol, scrubbers and drugs.

But deep down he's great, he's a bloody good mate,
And husband when alls done and said,
And on top of all this,
He lets me take the piss,
Without having once, punched my head.

So Tyrone today, we'd all like to say,
Happy birthday, and have many more.
It's been a long year,
Mixed with trauma and cheer.
But may happiness stay at your door.

Best present of the lot, is the one that you've got,
It's your Jo, who we know you adore
So we give you three cheers
Now you've made 40 years,
And hope you share many years more.

Paul and Joan - the wedding

It's the wedding day feast of the beauty and beast,
Who we all know as Joany and Paul,
And I do have to say in a round-about way,
It' a wonder it's happened at all.

But it has and were here and were drinking their beer,
So you can't say it's been a bad thing,
Tight fisted it aint and theres been no restraint,
Just look at the size of that ring!

But it's loving that counts, not money amounts,
When it comes down to tying the Knot,
And from what we have seen, (if you know what I mean),
Of that they've both got quite a lot.

So let's toast them today and hope that they may,
Have a good life together always,
And we'll ever be here to wish them good cheer,
Providing that somebody pays.

So we wish them god speed and all that they need,
As they start on their new life today,
A toast one and all to our friends Joan and Paul,
Good luck, hip, hip, hip and hooray.

Toad of the road

He sits behind the wheel,
A manic grin upon his face.
He's Topsy Toad of Oldnall Road
He'll put you in your place.

He turns the key and starts the car.
Now is the time to worry.
'Cos' Topsy Toad of Oldnall Road
Is really in a hurry.

Next the gears. Where is reverse?
He's sure that it was there.
Now Topsy Toad of Oldnall Road
Is pulling out his hair.

That Bloody Car! That Pile of Scrap!
He'll throw it down the tip.
It's Topsy Toad of Oldnall Road.
He's such a BLOODY DRIP.

(With apologies to K.Grahame -- Wind in the Willows.)
(© Chris Newey)

Cabe

Sombre dark eyed gentle deer,
Would that I could have you near,
Kitchen, bed, and drawing room,
Working on a wiring loom.

This passion has no darkling menace,
Yet liken it as 'Death in Venice'.
Alabaster marble maid,
I'll ever love you, everglade.

Your flash of anger let me see,
In rare mixed glances thrown to me.
Oh proudest, finest, best of girls,
Still rise above the Tavern's churls
Serenely go, whilst I look on.
And dream the dreams I live upon.
"Tread softly" as 'twas said before,
That I may dream one dream the more.

Oh, pretty pilgrim, fare-you-well,
Shine on my sweet, through joy and hell.
Still treat as equals love and pain,
Though we may never meet again.
I'll think of you when you are gone,
And rue how age doth steal from one,
Be happy where you choose to be,
But now and then; remember me.

Steve Mottram's 50th

So it's now come to pass,
Mottram's fifty at last,
Though he looks about twenty years more,
But I suppose that's because,
He drinks like he does,
And he eats like a ravenous whore.

I would think that if we,
Was washed out to sea,
And we both ended up castaway,
I bet he would eat,
Me right down to me feet,
And he knows I dont like it that way.

So now he is fifty,
But keeps himself nifty,
And is now a big part of our lives,
Many may doubt him,
But we wouldn't be without him,
Although I'd still lock up your wives.

I do have to tell,
That he's made our life hell,
With his constant bombardment of text,
They're not very funny,
They just cost him money,
And they all make us feel very vexed.

But he's shaped up today,
And I do have to say,
With this party he's done us all proud,
It's the best one he's had,
He's a bloody good dad,
And we'll now sing his praises out loud.
Good luck to you Steve,
We hope you receive,

27

Nice presents and all that you may,
You have done many things,
Put wind beneath wings,
And looked after our Jo on the way,

Happy birthday our mate,
Carry on at this rate,
And I might start to like you a bit,
And say to you cheers,
And buy you some beers,
And that's a right load of bullshit.

Let's lift up our glasses,
And hope as time passes,
You'll have many more days like this,
Hip hip hooray,
For our Stevie's birthday,

Now let's all get back on the piss...

Ed' and Lou's engagement party

For Lou and Ed' it must be said:
They don't rush into things,
While other 'do's' have gone ahead,
They've waited in the wings.

But at long last, it's come to pass,
He's asked her for her hand.
The long' awaited party',
The 'bloody awful band'.

They said; they'd have a party,
With good food, friends and beer.
The only thing that puzzles me,
Is why, they had it here!

I know, that this is all old hat,
But they are, a lovely pair,
And Ed's o.k. although he's fat,
And I wish that I'd been there.

But let us wish them all the best,
As they set out to wed,
They have, already stood the test,
Of camp and board and bed.

And when all your tomorrows come,
And other loves may fail,
I know; We, know; that unlike some,
Yours, will survive the trail.

Good luck to you, our Ed and Lou,
May love and fortune smile,
On you and your's for evermore,
And happiness the while.

Joey Bear's 30th

It's Joey-wowey's birfy-wirfy,
Isn't she a 'lucky cow',
And though she's flirty-dirty-thirty,
We still love her anyhow.

Towee-wowee as she knowee,
Wants to give her 30 bumps,
But Ty-ee-wy-ee he would kwy-ee,
And give poor Towee 30 thumps.

So he'll have to do-ee poo-ee,
With a kissee wissee, so;
Lift your glassy-wassies high,
And toasty-woasty dearest Jo.

Patrick

You're gone now Pat,
Swirling away among the whispers of my memories,
Many vestiges, snatches and glimpsed pieces of you,
I know will return to me in the years that I have left,
Images, of your quiet resolve and gentle manners.
Your wicked impish humour and sense of occasion,
The fine taste exhibited in every facet of your life.
Your fastidious nature and fiercely held integrity.
Your charm, temper and solitary reflective moods.
How we drank. How we loved the Luncheon Club.
How we privately howled with laughter you and I,
At the many antics of the valued Brian de Thame.
How quick you were to see humour in all things.
How crass I could be, How you liked me for it.
You were a private man, difficult to know.
'though I think I got to know you a little;
A little more than some perhaps.
What rare fun we had.
How I will miss you,

Me and Micky McCormack

Micky Mc Cormack I saw you today,
Sat in the sun with your stick,
And I thought to myself it's a hell of a day,
For a fellow to be out on the sick,
As I swept past in haste,
For I've now got the taste,
To work ten bloody hours on the trot,
It occurred to me then,
That it's not only ten,
And it's me that is losing the plot,
You know I've stopped drinking,
And it's got me to thinking,
What a rare lucky fellow I am,
Me girlfriend's a beauty,
But what with this duty,
She thinks that I don't give a dam,
I'm earning good money,
But you know it seems funny,
I still have a raft of a debt,
And although I've been busted,
It's not done and dusted,
The Revenue's not finished yet,
Me daughter she's sick,
And I feel such a prick,
That I don't get to see her enough,
And what leisure I get,
It's no pleasure I get,
For I've still got me feet in the trough,
I'm a changed man of course,
Since I laid off the sauce,
And now I remember me name,
Though there is the odd thing,
Like I no longer sing,
And a sunset; it don't look the same,
But it's no use to crying,
We're both of us dying,
And no-one knows who'll go first,

But when we get to hell,
The Ow'd Man he will tell,
Which one had the terrible thirst,
But I shall not relent,
For I must pay the rent,
And all other bills if I can,
But let me tell you,
That whatever I do,
The shit still keeps hitting the fan,
Me life is a mess,
And it's still full of stress,
And the thought of it all makes me sick,
Oh! Micky Mc Cormack,
I saw you today,
Just sat in the sun with your stick.

Mike - our friend

How can you be dead? Our dear, dear friend,
Our vibrant bumptious lively loveable mate,
You were ever going to be there for us to send,
You up about your DIY but now it's too late.

To let you know how we really thought of you,
How loved you were by everyone you ever met,
With fondness amusement and admiration too,
A kind man, who all who knew would not forget.
A sensitive talented man who loved to please,
Who always made us welcome in your home,
And when there, always put us at our ease,
And had a way to say, 'I'm glad you've come'.

We'll miss you, but we're glad that your brief pain,
Passed quickly, though it flickered out that light,
Perhaps now you will play your violin again,
And share with other souls the great delight.

A saying is to; "Never let anything go unsaid",
There are things we didn't say; and now you're dead,
Incredulous now, our tears for you are shed,
How, our dear, dear friend, can you be dead!

A Gornal Gourmet Evening

"Oh do come to Dinner" said Julie and Taff,
We'll do something special and all have a 'laff',
So Timothy and Susan and Joanne and Tye,
Said "that's an idea let's just give it a try".

And so they set off on that ill-fated day,
Deciding to stop for a drink on the way,
At a Pub almost giving the spirits away,
So if you drank a lot there was little to pay.

And of course they all drank at a hell of a rate,
And of course they arrived in a 'bit of a state',
When Jo said to Tye don't you spoil this for me,
He said "fuck off" and just gave her the 'V'.

So then he knocked over his first glass of wine,
The first one of several and, this was a sign,
Of more things to come dear readers you know,
You've heard nothing yet of this sad tale of woe.

He then tried to eat when he found he was able,
To just reach a plate which was centre of table,
And came the main course well deserving a pat,
All he could mutter was "what the fucks that?"

And as he slumped over, Jo said "Tyrone please,
You've fallen asleep with your hand in the cheese",
Then he blundered away using gestures erratic,
And was much later found comatose in the attic.

Sue noticed then Tim was away from his place,
And found him and Julie both sucking some face,
She pulled them asunder and with a loud sob,
Said "Bastard" and gave Tim a smack in the gob.

They all then attempted to save the sad night,
In spite of the fact they were terribly tight,
  When Julie said "anyone like a bit more?"
Sue gave her a dig and she fell on the floor.

Taff seemed to perceive a degree of distress,
But elected to giggle his way through the mess,
A decision was made then to leave all this grub,
And - would you believe it- go back to the pub.

Sue said to a neighbour as she passed the gate,
"I'd lock up your husband if I was you mate",
And so they deserted, these *wonderful guests'*,
To leave the host's house in a terrible mess.

With wine on the tablecloth food on the floor,
A scene of destruction, well who could want more,
Stretched out in a thin line they all headed south,
Each girl often belting their bloke in the mouth.

Thank God! That amid all this horror and choss,
Old "Mushee" arrived like a Knight on an 'Oss',
He scooped them all up and carried them here,
Still covered in red wine, blood, vodka and beer.

The moral of course: If you don't want a night,
With insults and mayhem a binge and a fight,
But want to remember the night as a winner,
Whatever you do DON'T HAVE THIS LOT TO DINNER!

Mystery Lady 2

May I beseech thee now my dearest dear,
To grant the dalliance soon for which I pray,
Lest those dark days of which I ever fear,
Do come to shake the darling buds of May.

Maura's 60th

Dear Maura, or Mary, or Moira, or Mo',
Which one is the right one, we'd all like to know,
For it's very confusing for some of us here,
Who are eating your food and imbibing your beer.

Now I know it don't matter to what you're called,
Like it doesn't to Taff when they say that he's bald,
Or to Spiv, or to Swiv, or to Bennie, or Tat,
And yes, I'm aware that they call me a pratt!

But the point I'm making it doesn't seem right,
That we all will go out at the end of the night,
Us all thanking you kindly in a different name,
And well I don't know, but it just seems a shame.

The confusion there'll be when we're all of us gone,
That only a few of us said the right one,
The ones that I mean of course happen to be,
Your immediate family, Like Francis and me.

But what am I saying, does it matter at all,
Providing you always respond to the call,
Of Maura, or Mary, or Moira, or Mo,
For you'll always be loved by the people you know.

And you're sixty today and we'd all like to say,
How much we all love you in every way,
However you say it its perfectly clear,
You're one lovely person and everyone here.

Will say happy birthday and want you to know,
That whatever you're called and wherever you go,
Well remembers to greet you just simply as so,
Hail Mary…or Maura…or Moira…or Mo!

Mystery Lady 3

There was a girl we loved you know,
And now she's beastly dead,
But she had love for everyone,
And she looked good in red,
And now she's gone,
And we are poor,
That we will no more see,
That girl, our girl,
The lovely pearl,
The way she used to be.

Frank Furlong's 65th - 2007

Francis me lad, we're all awful glad that you've made it to age sixty five,
For what you've been through, if half of its true, you really should not be alive,
You've been battered and bruised and often abused and had a most colourful life,
From riches to rags, from cigars to fags but you still have your wonderful wife.

We'd just like to say, that we'd give without pay our friendship to you and we do,
For if we were in trouble, we'd get it back double and that is most certainly true,
You've a few little flaws and you break a few laws but what consternation is this,
You smoke far too much, which is only a crutch and you're constantly out on the piss.

But you're always good fun and always the one to laugh in the face of adversity,
You take all on the chin and mostly you win. That was one bloody good university,
You're the one bloke that we just all like to see whenever we enter the room,
For we know at our meeting we'll get a good greeting without any sadness or gloom.

You're now sixty five and we hope that you thrive for many more years left to come,
We wish you good cheer, keep drinking the beer along with the "Lambs Navy Rum",
You know that we love you, there's no one above you in matters concerning the pub,
If there's a small fiddle, your there in the middle, the main man, the master, the hub.

So let's toast you today and let us all pay you the homage you richly deserve,
Lord bless you our friend may God always send the things that you wish to preserve,
Memories like these and the people you please the ones you have known for so long,
Happy Birthday to you and many more too. Raise your glasses to Francis Furlong.

Jo and Tye (The Farewell)

We're all gathered here with mixed feelings I know,
For although we like good food and beer.
What we none of us like is to lose Tye and Jo,
They're two people we hold very dear.

We've shared so much with a mixture of sorrow,
But it's mostly been good for us all,
And I'm sure that whatever life holds for tomorrow,
This decision will be a good call.

We had ups we had downs and applauses and boos,
 Marriages, funerals and luncheons,
Christmases, discotheques, fancy dress do's,
In fact we've had all sorts of functions.

And Jo's handled them all with a shrug and a smile,
And even when things turned out shit!
She'd try something new with her typical style,
And her truly remarkable grit,

And with many memories they'll leave us in full,
Which will bring a fond smile to one's face,
Like once when old Tyrone got out of his skull,
And proceeded to smash up the place.

The pub trades a tough one and that is a fact,
And it's brought not a few to their knees,
But you both have your love and a marriage intact,
And a whole lot of future to seize.

So here's to you both for always we'll love you,
You'll never be far from our thought,
For us there is no-one who could be above you,
For a friendship which cannot be bought.

Good luck and God bless you wherever you go,
We know that in future we'll meet,
With lovely Tyrone and our beautiful Jo,
Cos you'll only be just down the street.

Ron Mansfield's 60th

Dearest Ron, we had to 'Con' you into coming here
It was the only way to stop you from buying all the beer
For if we'd met you up the road we know you'd never let
Us have a chance to buy a round you're such a generous 'Get'

But now that we have got you here I know I speak for all
In saying that you always make big problems look so small
With failing health and waning wealth you never lost your humour
Despite the fact that we once thought that "It Could Be a Toomer"

Financially, emotionally, the things that you've been through
Like falling deep and deeper still into the 'Doggie Do'
But you were always there for us and managed all the while
To keep that rare ability to make your old friends smile

So now we're here to drink the beer and celebrate this day
That you have caused to happen in the good Old Mansfield way
So here's to you. Its sixty years of many joys and sorrows
We hope that you enjoy today and many more tomorrows

Oh by the way where's Roger? cos he always likes a laugh
I s'pose it doesn't matter if you haven't brought your scarf
Happy Birthday Ronald and remember we'll love you
Not just on your 60th but all the whole year through

Return

It's half past six,
And I am pissed,
And happy so to be Sir,
For in this state,
I cannot hate,
And always,
I'm in love Sir,
I love the dawn,
I love my dog,
I love the light I see Sir,
I love the fact,
That I'm alive,
And happy so to be Sir.

Ben and Lou's 50th

Dearest Steven and Lucile,
- Or can we call you Ben and Lou -
We're mustered here to drink your beer,
And wish you happy birthday too,
This poem should have been a breeze,
To say nice things about you two,
And one I thought I'd do with ease,
But I just didn't have a clue,
And then I thought hang on a bit,
 There must at least be some good shit,
And so there is and plenty too,
And we would like to say to you,
We love you both and wouldn't be,
 Without your vibrant company,
For every time there is a do,
You're always there to see it through,
Your kindly helpful cheerful muckers,
And not like lots of other people,
You're always there to lend a hand,
To listen and to understand,
You're both despite a deal of strife,
Integral parts to all our life,
Ben's a solid constant friend,
Who'll be there for you in the end,
And though Lou is a sometime Diva,
We'd not change one hair on her beaver,
For mostly when she has a whinge,
She's on about one's lesbian fringe,
And if what's needed is a mate,
You are without a doubt first rate,
We toast you now and wish you well,
And many years to come as well,
And now you're two score years and ten,
HAPPY BIRTHDAY LOU and BEN

Charlie's birthday - 2009

Sweet birthday girl I gaze at you,
As winter must look oft' on spring,
Reflecting that first green of youth,
For me the sad lost lovely thing,
And how my love, I long to be,
In that good place you occupy,
This thing I fear can never be,
Still I will love you till I die.
If I could tear the veil of time,
To travel back and be with you,
Would you be happy to be mine,
I reckon about a week'll do.

Farewell Maggie

Eina fugle apple strudel,
Ich mine little flugel horn,
Eisner shtiner sausage viner,
Daschund und der Matter Horn,
Donner Blitzen veenal shlitzen,
Liebfraumilch und vintervane,
Maggie mien da Frau Gluvine,
Danker und Aulfuidazane

And for you Englanders...?

Dearest Maggie we will miss you,
For you're now a family part,
When you're gone there'll be a void,
In every bodies life and heart,
We've seen you happy seen you sad,
Seen you drunk and seen you mad,
Seen you worried seen you glad,
But no one's ever seen you bad,
To us you'll always be the one,
Who mispronounces *sree und von*,
But yet you smile when you appear,
In every way you bring us cheer,
And there can never be one who,
Lights up a room just quite like you,
So when you're gone remember this,
Or should I say, remember 'zis',
There'll always be a welcome here,
For someone who we hold so dear,
So promise us that you'll come back,
To friendship you will never lack,
To love for you so strong and steady,
That we are missing you already,
So goodbye Maggie May for now,
And Cassie too a fond "Bow Wow",

Good luck, God bless in all you do,
Let's pray that you'll be happy too,
Let's toast you now and say Ta Ra,
To Maggie Dear "Hip Hip Hoorah!"

Jenny

(One year at The Station Inn - June 2009)

Jenny dear it's been a year since you arrived to please us
And carried out some miracles just like that good bloke Jesus.
With the help of loving friends, your husband son and daughter
You have proved to all of us that you can walk on water.

You bustled in and cleaned us up and brought the custom back
And keep us here with well-kept beer the friendship and the crack.
Your lovely staff all greet us with a welcome warmth and wit
But insisting Dan goes topless though is stretching it a bit.

You've got some lovely people of whom we're very fond,
And one of them is Sadie and Brother Is she blonde!
She helped us do a crossword and one clue was "young bear"
And giving lots of thought to this what she put down was "care,"

The job you've got's a tough one and that we all can see
But you've got time for every one, like you had time for me
And you are very pretty, also pretty nice and clever,
And we all love you "Jenny Wren" and hope you stay for ever.

So lift your glasses one and all and toast the year just gone,
And toast the wish that your success will just go on and on,
And toast the hope that in this pub you'll make a pretty penny
And most of all lets toast the love we hold for our dear Jenny.

Julie's recovery

Julie dear, we're gathered here, to say how glad we are,
That you've made such a 'come back just like a movie star,
With lots of grit, through all that shit, and just a little panic,
You're back to show us all that your lifeboat is no 'Titanic'.

To have you here, to drink your beer and have a quiet laff,
Must be the best thing for you yet, apart from meeting Taff,
He must have been, as we have seen a comfort every day,
One day you must explain to me, what is he trying to say?

So here's to you and Peter too long may your love endure,
I hoped to have such happiness but for me there is no cure,
Your home again and free from pain a Pilgrim back with us,
A toast to you our Julie, now; let's gives you lots of fuss.

"Lady Sadie" - Christmas 2009

Lovely Sadie we love you,
In everything you say and do,
So seldom do we see you down,
And never do we see you frown,
Perhaps you sometimes cry alone,
But that to us will not be known,
You are so fine and lithe and blonde,
And one of whom we're very fond,
So never let our mocking way ,
Change anything of what you say,
Because you are a vital part,
Of all our love and life and heart,
And all our teasing will not mar,
For "Beautiful" is what you are,
Don't ever let your sweetness falter,
Or someone dare to make you alter,
And always if you can somehow,
Remain the way that you are now,
For one who loves you if you knew,
Now writes this poem just for you.

Mystery Lady 4

See how this bracelet,
Encompasses thy wrist,
So doth thy breast ,
Encloseth my poor heart,
Wear them both sweet lady,
For both of them are thine.

Nikki's 40th

Nikki Elizabeth Wright,
Being 40 gives one such a fright,
I ought to know,
About ten years ago,
It happened to me. Yes that's right.

But to see you today,
I do have to say,
That you just haven't altered at all,
From the girl who I took,
Thanking God for my luck,
To the old pigeon fanciers ball,

You're as lovely and scatty today,
As you were on your great wedding day,
You arrived in a state,
About half an hour late,
Like Timothy does every way,

But you still are the best,
Above all the rest,
When it comes down to being a friend,
When the corner is tight,
Just call Nikki Wright,
She'll be there for you in the end,

So lift up your glasses,
(I said glasses not arses),
Let's drink to our girls 40 years,
Happy Birthday to you,
And many more too,
"To Nikki, Best Wishes and CHEERS"

Sara's tool shed inauguration - 2009

All hail! To this sweet edifice serene,
That never yet a spade or fork has seen,
We gather now in praise and awe to see,
Dear Sara's shed which took so long to be.
And as we gaze in pride yet still we know,
Another place where she could stick her hoe,
And here he is, the man we all knew could
Build her this 'little palace' made of wood.
It would have been much earlier, we think,
If he'd stopped nipping next door for a drink.
But credit where it's due to Chris our friend,
For building sheds his talent has no end,
And this one all will say is up to scratch,
But for the one next door it has no match.
So lift your glasses now and toast the day,
In that 'shed opening' customary way,
For more nice words to say we are agropin'
Let's just declare this bloody tool shed; Open.

Susan's 60th

Sexy Susan now you're sixty,
So we'd like to say to you,
We simply love you Sexy Susan,
Stacks of us will say so too,
You are super Sexy Susan,
So your super husband said,
Since he saw you were so sexy,
Said he simply had to wed,
Several something years ago,
Or so he said to me he said,
He wasn't sorry that he said so,
He could slither in your bed.
Since so many smashing years,
Seem to you as centuries now,
Still surviving smiles and tears,
See you safe and sound somehow,
So we'll sincerely say to you,
This Sunday in this special way,
Scholl, Shlaint, Skal, Saud and Salud,
Sweet Susan, have a Smashing day.

Taff's 50th

Dear Taff, it's today, that you've found your way,
To the dreaded half century affair,
And though you're turned fifty - you look pretty nifty,
Of course that's apart from the hair.

But we'd all like to say that in every way,
We love you the way that you are,
We know you'd drive miles - just to share a few smiles,
If they'd just let you loose with a car.

And over the years and through hundreds of beers,
You've become very close to our heart,
And a person that we - are just happy to see,
Even though you're a bit of a tart.

And you are a good ref being blind daft and deaf,
And I do have a fond memory,
When they all shouted that - this referee is a twat,
I said who called the twat a referee.

But I do have to state that he's been a good mate,
To me and to many more here,
He's always been there - with a kindness to share,
And we all will hold him very dear.

So let's toast him hearty and thanks for the party,
We hope you have many more years,
Madly and truly - just like you love Julie,
Peter, we love you, happy birthday and Cheers!

Teresa and Andy – congrat's and thanks...

Tree' and And', please understand, we haven't lost the plot,
We didn't misremember - we simply just forgot,
To bring your wedding present on the proper day,
But never mind 'cos here it is and we'd just like to say,
Thank you for the invite and thank you for the fun,
And thank you for the time we had in the evening sun,
You both looked so fantastic and we will not forget,
It was the bestest wedding we have ever been to yet,
The venue and the ambience the weather food and wine,
The people and the music which made the day so fine,
And when at first I saw you I thought what a lovely pair,
And Andy looked OK as well...if he only had some hair!

So many thanks for having us and we all wish that you,
Will have a happy wedded life and all your dreams come true,
Good luck to you and all you want we hope will come your way,
And may the magic stay for you as on your wedding day.

Bonfire Night at the Webster's - 2010

We're here at The Webster's for fireworks and fun,
And I know that the evening has hardly begun,
But a chance to say thank you must never be missed,
Before everyone gets a little too hysterical.

And note as you do through the garden parade,
Embellishments that our two hosts have had made,
The sunburst of course would be one such a treat,
If it hadn't been trampled with our muddy feet.

The sheds still resplendent for those who don't know,
That I wrote about those simply ages ago,
Extensions and patios improvements galore,
I could go on all night but you'd think me a bore.

More importantly though and I think you'll agree,
There's the great hospitality we always see,
When Sara and Chris give us such a great time,
They deserve a bit more than a crummy old rhyme.

So thanks to you both from me and the gang,
And let's hope that this evening will end with a bang,
And I do hope it does because as you all know,
The last one that I had was a few weeks ago.

But let things commence let's get on with the night,
There are rockets and bangers and sparklers to light,
But let's give these two just the best of all toasts,
To Sara and Chris just the best of all hosts.

Charlie's 21st birthday – 2010.

Dearest Charlie now you are,
The loveliest twenty one year star,
And though your life has but begun,
Please know that still, this aged sun,
Though dull with time and faded hue,
Still fondly gazes down on you,
And when oft in your company,
The heavenly body that I see,
That shades all others dear is thine,
Which nothing can or will outshine,
So 'Happy Birthday' pretty girl,
And always be the lovely pearl,
We see today at twenty one,
And let your happiness go on,
And take this rhyme as my poor gift,
Though try I may to show my drift,
I guess the world will never see,
A poem lovelier than thee.

Lofty's 60th

Dearest Bob you made the day, although you nearly 'muffed it',
Most of us had thought by now you really should have 'snuffed it',
But you have always had the way of showing us you're right -
At quizzes, quotes and crosswords...even when you're very tight!
And boy! We're glad that your still here, we hope for very long,
To just keeping on telling Webster that he's always in the wrong,
And moan about old Alice, though no-one could ever match her,
She's the nicest girl who ever lived, apart from Margaret Thatcher,
You've given us all so much value and fine memories to keep,
It's hoped that while I'm reading this you're not stood up asleep,
You have been a great companion who we love to have around,
Just keep telling Chris Webster that it's time he bought a round,
And you and I have been good old friends as anyone can see,
Apart from when I jumped up once and punched you on the knee,
And here you are come sixty now and still looking pretty good,
You're sexy, slim and single too which is much misunderstood,
We all know that you will say to us that there is just nothing to it,
But what everyone would say to that is how you bloody do it,
But any way God Bless you mate we are here to wish you well,
So it's happy birthday Loftus dear and have many more as well,
Now let's all lift our glasses to this man to toast his sixtieth year,
And quickly get back to the bar before he drinks up all the beer.

Mike Anthill - Memorial

We're all here again for a wonderful day,
To remember Old Mike in the usual way,
But while we're carousing and supping the beer,
Let's remember the ones who are no longer here.

Mike Dalziel, Harry Hickman, John Preston and Ray,
Who shared their lives with us in every way,
I'm sure that this day will be one from now on,
When we drink to our friends who are now sadly gone.

And still to remember a wonderful man,
Who some will remember like most of us can,
As kindly and loving and funny and good,
He'd be running this function if only he could.

He liked playing golf with the people he knew,
And doing those things that we loved him to do,
Like drink with us think with us sing with us too,
And that's what we miss and his weaknesses too.

Like solving the crosswords that he held so dear,
While completely forgetting to order the beer,
Or listening to customer's grumbles and gripes,
But completely forgetting to clean out the pipes.

He would pay for an outing including the grub,
In spite of the fact that it emptied his pub,
He was generous and loving and giving and broke,
Was there ever was such a remarkable bloke?

He could play a guitar just like ringing a bell,
And knock up a curry that was hotter than hell,
In fact he once made one he wanted to sell us,
The only thing was, he'd forgotten to tell us.

Still we will remember him every year,
On this day in August and might shed a tear,
But mostly we'll smile and we'll toast him in beer,
"Mike Antill and others". We wish you were here.

Two years at The Station

Another year and you'r still here and we're so very glad,
It mostly was a happy one but sometimes it was sad,
Whatever this pub throws at you, you take it on the chin,
And rise to all occasions hiding sorrow with a grin.

And we all see how tough it is to run a place like this,
So please try to forgive us when we often take the piss,
And also know we love you all as no doubt you can tell,
Marcus, Sam and Bud the dog, that tasty bird as well.

And we all hope you'll be around for many, many years,
To give us your good company and sell us your good beers,
And keep them gnomes a'commin always put us to the test,
For we all love you Jenny Wren, you simply are the best.

Instead of a Bottle

(Having been invited to one of Roger Gear's fine parties the
abstemious author brought beans.)

Had I the heaven's embroidered cloths,
Inwrought with golden and silver light,
The blue and the dim and the dark cloths
Of night and light and the half-light,
I would spread the cloths under your feet;
But I being poor have only my beans;
I have spread beans under your feet;
Tread softly because you tread on my beans.

(a beautiful work wrecked by T.S .Aug' 2010)

Bonfire Night at the Webster's - 2011

We're all here tonight at the Webster's locality,
To enjoy yet again their renowned hospitality,
They had hoped for rain for I know that they're 'itchin',
To have everyone see their shiny new kitchen.

The 'Glitterati' are here and that includes me,
And so many old faces that I love to see,
There's Carbide and Doody and Lulu and Ron,
And if I'm not mistaken there goes 'Kelly Lunn'.

I know that the night will be as always is,
With fine food and fireworks and frolics and fizz,
With fair friends and fountains and fondues and fears,
And try saying that when you've had a few beers .

Let's hope this tradition will last a long time,
It gives me a platform for my crummy rhyme,
And I know that we all so look forward to this,
It gives us a chance to get out on the drink.

So thank you again to our Sara and Chris,
And thank you again for giving us this,
And please be assured that it's not just a platitude,
As we all applaud now to show you our gratitude.

Chris Webster's 60th - 2012

A poem that I penned just a decade ago,
Told of Chris when of course he was fifty,
It spoke in amazement that he had survived,
But the bastards still here and he's sixty.

It just goes to show if you care for your health,
And just have the occasional drink,
And work out a lot and jog to the car,
You'll last longer than most people think.

We're glad he's still here and sharing his beer,
And to many he's proved a true friend,
And we love him a lot even when he's a pain,
And starts driving us all round the bend.

When he and I met such a long while ago,
It's a very long time we go back,
He had hair on his face and lots on his head,
And what's more I believe it was black.

If you know him you love him it's true,
And many stories about him abound,
Eccentric and odd and really quite bright,
But his quality is; that he's sound.

So here's to you Chris in your sixty-first year,
May your merriment go on and on,
We toast you today and give you a cheer,
For the many good things that you've done.

Charlie Powell's 50th

We like Charlie Powell,
He's a bloody good sort,
He likes all types of things,
Like sex, drinking and sport.
And when not indulging,
Or playing or romancing,
He gets on the dance floor,
And he calls it dancing.
It's not much of a dance,
It's more like a hop,
And what's worse I've discovered,
His dad was a cop.
He was called Copper Powell,
And it has to be said,
When I was a youngster,
He once punched my head..
But I bet I deserved it,
For something I'd done.
Copper Powell was a good man,
A lot like his son - who is 50 today,
Or at least very near.
So we'll all raise our glasses,
And toast him in beer,
So here's to you Charlie,
Your half century in life.
And here's to poor Nancy,
Your long suffering wife.
Happy birthday dear Charlie,
We'd all like to say;
We hope you have many,
Returns of the day.

Frank Furlong's 70th

Dearest Frank we'd like to thank you just for being you,
And we Aurra thank dear Maura for things that she's done too,
But now you have made seventy and no-one thought you would,
The chances you'll make eighty now we think are pretty good.

So happy birthday our dear friend and thank you for your presence,
And I for one am happy that you didn't want any presents,
And thank you for this party and thank you for the fun,
And I'll write a better poem next when you are seventy one.

Mystery Lady 5

Had I but time my dear to answer thee correct,
And have the space to sure our fond respect,
As much would we our loving words resume,
And diverse feasts of love and art consume.

Had but the languorous leisure then to hand,
When then the wit had in that erstwhile land,
I'd mastered time and space to give it sway,
But now that keeper time, doth tell me nay.

And had but strength to leave the cup alone,
Still lending blame to others, yet bemoan,
That time that once I had to tend the quaff,
Was stolen from which time had I enough.

When I could while away the languid year,
Neglecting much that should be held so dear,
Yet so grim Nemesis doth now call for her due,
Seldom stray my thoughts dear love from you.

Mick Lown's 60th

Dearest Mick Lown you're a man of renown,
And now you are 60 poor man,
Not a bad thing to be, it happened to me,
Remember last year if you can.

But I'd quite like to say, that in every way,
You've become a big part of our life,
A mate and a mucker, a really good friend,
With your very long suffering wife.

Your humour is dry and although I still try,
To outwit you whenever I can,
I have to confess I'm a giggling mess,
When faced with your witty 'deadpan'.

All love you this minute. It's your 60th innit,
So we hope you will have a good time,
And what you will bring, if you do play and sing,
Will be better than this crummy rhyme.

Happy Birthday dear mate we know you will hate,
The place Father Time will now shove you,
But what you can say, is on this happy day,
You're surrounded by people who love you.

Billy Taylor's 60th Birthday Bash

Now Billy your 60 it's come up at last,
And we're all gathered here just to gloat.
You've done us all right, to give us this night,
And you've finally pushed out the boat.

We hope you'll have many, I was saying to Penny,
There's a poem to write about Bill,
She said you'll be fine, make it better than mine,
You can and you probably will.

But Billy we love you, there's no-one above you,
You're constant and kind and sincere,
Wherever you meet us, whenever you greet us,
You always do so with good cheer.

Even when tight, you're incredibly bright,
In the quizzes and all crossword too,
At maths not so grand, but you do understand,
How to take at least one tooth from two.

Whenever you roam, it's to your second home,
And to everyone's great admiration,
We know where you are, and don't have to look far,
You will only be round at the Station.

But tonight is your night, and we think you're alright,
For you are a big part of our life,
You are a dear friend, and our best thoughts we send,
To you and to Jane your poor wife.

So let's drink with you, like we always do,
And wish you have many more years,
So we can all please, have a lot more of these,
Happy Birthdays dear William and "cheers".

Steve Mottram's 60th

So Steven your sixty and I do have to say,
That the years, they do really mount up,
But if I could be bold you look very old,
And I think you should have a count up.

But not being hasty cos you can look tasty,
Although it's got to be in the dark,
A wow with the ladies like the devil in Hades,
Like your trips late at night to the park.

A thing without fear is that you are loved here,
There is nobody here who would doubt you,
And most of the fun that needs to be done,
This just wouldn't function without you.

Your organisation and your fraternisation,
Is unequalled by anyone here,
If there's things to do, we all look to you,
And we know you'll be there it is clear.

So let's wish you well and let us all dwell,
On the goodness that you have brought here,
The golf and the fun the heaven and the hell,
And especially tonight, the free beer.

Although sixty is sad you are a good dad,
And I think that all here would agree,
You are a good mucker and a really good friend,
Happy birthday to our great mate Stevie.

Penny

In this pub we have a lass,
Who is admired by many.
She's good and kind,
And all will find,
There's no-one like "Our Penny".

She works so hard but yet she has,
The time to chat and hear,
All the quips,
From all the drips,
Who stand and guzzle beer.

Even at a busy time,
She handles things with ease,
And does her stuff,
Without rebuff,
To banter or to tease.

She really is a classy act,
And puts us in our place,
When all we need,
Is just to heed,
That look upon her face.

We would not be without her,
Without her we'd be sad,
For when we sup,
And she turns up,
This Penny's not so bad,

So here's to you our dearest Pen',
We all love you because,
You simply are,
The best by far,
There is, and ever was.

Tone and Karen's wedding

The time has come hip hip hooray,
For Tone and Karen's happy day,
And now instead of spinning discies,
And pulling pints and selling whiskeys,
And sipping drinks designed to cripple,
Like his old favourite 'slippery nipple',
And showing folks how to behave,
At wedding, function, dance or rave.

And watching horses always lose,
Just like that football team the blues,
And telling how to hold a bat,
(Not that he's very good at that),
He can sit back with great distain,
And watch his friends take all the strain.

There are many things he likes to do,
And both of us like swimming too,
His pulling power is hardly barren,
If he can get a girl like Karen,
At first I thought she'd have to settle,
Close second best to ' heavy metal',
But Karen no, don't be upset,
For him you're just the best thing yet.

We wish you happiness and health,
And peace and love and warmth and wealth,
So to you both let glasses raise,
To Tone and Karen; happy days.

Susan's 59th

Dearest Sue we all love you and we're all here to show it,
With all your friends and family here I guess by now you know it,
So now it is your birthday we wish you many more,
I'm told that you are forty three but I think forty four,
There's one thing I would like to say before I get too pissed,
That you have got the bestest tits that I have ever kissed,
So happy birthday Susan enjoy the evening's fun,
And we would like to toast you raise glasses everyone.

Ian Thomson remembered...

I only knew Ian for about the last twenty years of his life,
But to know him was to love him,
He always reminded me of a P.G. Wodehouse character.

I remember once when someone came into the pub and enquired:
"Is anybody going anywhere near Brierly Hill tomorrow?"
He said: "Good Lord; I would hardly have thought so – no!"

And sometimes he was forgetful and would use substitute words,
In place of the ones that he had forgotten,

A few years ago, one of the licensees at our local ,
Left to take over 'The Fighting Cocks at Romsley',
And when he popped in to see us a few weeks later,
Ian said to him: "Hello Mark, how are you getting on,
At "The Squabbling Doo Dha's"

He was a nice man with many friends,
And as his good friends go there can be no better example,
Than Chris Webster who gave him so much support,
And invaluable assistance during the last few painful months of his
life.

For me Ians legacy is will be;
That whenever or wherever you found yourself in his company,
The experience was always enjoyable,
He was a kind man with a ready wit and a great sense of fun,
We were always pleased to see him,
And these are not bad memories to leave behind.

Our Lord Thomson;
We loved you - we will miss you - we will remember you.

Sara's 60th

Dearest Sara you are 60 - though no-one would ever know,
For to us you're young and ageless and the nicest girl we know,
All the things that you put up with shows to us that you're a saint,
And I think we all agree it's something that your husband aint,
So gentle lady happy birthday to a girl we all adore,
And we assembled all now wish you many, many, many more.

The Hit

I ride my cab from dawn to dusk,
As cabbies do as cabbies must,
But what I love I must admit,
Is the longed for evening hit.

There was a time that it would do,
To have a pint of beer or two,
But now I know that will not do,
It takes a weeley dwinky poo.

Arriving home and feeling raw,
One won't do cos I need four,
And when I do I feel so great,
That soon I find it moves to eight.

But eights no good it's just a jot,
And really doesn't hit the spot,
So on I go and feel like shit,
But God, don't take away that hit.

Warren and Lynn the Wedding

Dear Warren and Lynn we think it's a sin,
That you've kept us all waiting so long,
To see you both wed but it has to be said,
That a rushed thing will often go wrong.

You've talked quite a lot about tying the knot,
And you thought it would be a good plan,
But you've been so immersed in wanting things first,
Like a nice house a car and a clan.

But now you've got those it's time I suppose,
To get with the rest of the gang,
You might just as well, come and join us in hell,
(I mean marriage of course, that's just slang).

They met in a wine bar one memorable night,
Where Warren spilt drink on Lynn's dress,
Which he then tried to mop, till she told him to stop,
And said; "most of that's me! More or less".

And it went on from there they became a nice pair,
And their love for each other just shone,
It was all heart to heart to heart they were never apart,
Except when the rugby was on.

When all's said and done, they have always had fun,
And their love has remained undiminished,
And they put all the best into building their nest,
After each rugby season had finished.

But now we're all here to wish them good cheer,
And many good years spent together,
The smiles and the frowns the ups and the downs,
The journey through foul and fair weather.

You both will come through like always you do,
As fine friends a good father and mother,
And you'll have a great life as a husband and wife,
With the good love you have for each other.

So come lads and lassies and lift up your tassies,
And toast, if you still find the room,
The finest of folk to whom these words were spoke,
To Lynn and to Warren, the Bride and the Groom!

Sixty-five

Lord let me be your supplicant in everything I say and do,
And let me be a happy man and to my loving friends be true,
And let me have few more years and also Lord a few more beers,
And so that I can feel alive a few more laughs and fewer tears,
The lottery? Well I don't care as long as I can keep my hair...

Requiem (Martin Tomlinson – March 2000)

There has not been sufficient time,
For us to mourn the passing of our friend,
And time it takes ,
For me and she and we,
To bring it to an end,
And when we do ,
Still we will not forget,
The gentle man,
Who we are glad we met.

Topsy's 65th birthday

As I was going up the stair,
I saw a friend, I stopped to stare,
I wondered that he'd changed no more,
On having passed – just sixty-four.

From here and now your new life starts,
Look forward now, forget the past,
A man mature you can yet thrive,
You're not old yet! - just sixty-five.

Perhaps it's time to give up work,
I don't suggest that you should shirk,
But would your punters let you leave?
Not half a chance I do believe.

The calls come in by day and night,
The desperate ones begin to fight,
We need our lifts, we must, we can,
Now where on earth's that nice young man?

And so it seems you're here to stay,
And ferry people through the day,
The love your warmth, your charm, your wit,
This bed you've made so lie on it.

We all can look into your past,
Fond memories all made to last,
More fun we'll have in years ahead,
Of that we're sure, - take it as read.

Our rhyming effort can't compare,
To the Masters skill and flair,
Still this verse we now do send,
As bestest wishes to our friend.

(© Chris Webster)

There is a girl...

There is a girl, who in the dreary tenor of my day,
Shines like a sun, amid the milling dullard stars,
And glimmers like the diamond gem of May,
Outbrights the Taverns tawdry paste by far.

And when she nightly comes to court,
Her courtiers to see,
I would the way she looks at them,
That she would look at me.

But only with amusement,
Does she rarely glance my way,
And I the tool will play the fool,
For homage I must pay.

Oh lovely lady, dreadful tart,
Know you not you have my heart,
But for one moment let me see,
The lingered look which stays for me.

The Stationers

Tony Smith, Tony Smith.
Is it fact or is it myth?
You are a Smith we are told.
But is it black or is it gold?

         Taff, Taff,
         Oh what a gaff.
         Too Much wine,
         Now a ban and a fine

                  Mark, Mark.
                  Up with the lark.
                  Farming's no fun
                  Always work to be done.

Liz, Liz.
The "champagne" of Fizz.
From her boots to her hair
She puts the fine in "finefayre".

         Bev and Chris.
         A couple hard to miss.
         He has got a chinful of hair.
         Bev has not, what a fine pair!

                  Steve, Steve.
                  I do believe,
                  Drives his cab round the Minster,
                  Searching for a likely spinster.

Stan, Stan.
Plays with élan,
Better by far,
Just to play a guitar.

         Jo and Tye,
         Doesn't time fly
         Very soon we hear
         You'll be married a year.

(© Chris Newey - 2001)

Lost Threads

Much of our past has ebbed away,
The 'Brinton's Bull' no more,
Will bellow out the call to work,
Which work there was to call us for.

The clanging Drop Forge hammers,
Which woke us in our bed,
Are silent too and likely they who,
Worked the hammers now are dead.

The 'Sugar Factory' is no more,
With its sweet and Beety smells,
No whitening billows now enshroud,
The gaunt grey empty silo shells.

How many gone of down town pubs,
Where we could drink our fill,
'The old 'Black Bull' and 'Worcester Cross',
The sorely missed; 'Green Man and Still'.

The majestic old gasometer,
Its sulphur smell of coal and of tar,
Has disappeared, and in its stead;
Some ghastly sort of 'Burger Bar'.

Shawled and sepia tinted gypsies,
Selling pegs from door to door,
Cursing when we didn't buy them,
Do not call on us the more.

No chlorine muffled noises now,
At Kidderminster's swimming pool,
Where Mr Padfield loudly blew,
His whistle when we played the fool,

Where are the groups of gossips gone,
Who gathered by the garden gates,
And shrieked and cackled endlessly,
'bout laundry, kids and other hates.

The Rag and Bone man calls no more,
With his incoherent cry,
Swopping clothes for day old chicks,
Which all within a week would die.

And snot nosed kids from council houses,
Pushing old prams filled with coke,
To cheaply fuel the sooty fires,
That filled their Spartan homes with smoke.

The fond remembered Whitsuntide,
With Church Parades and tooting bands,
And lorry loads of waving kids,
With sticky chocolate covered hands.

And Bantocks horses plod no more,
From Marlborough street to Station Hill,
And down again with sparking hooves,
To test the drivers braking skill.

Gone are the shouting traders too,
From Kidderminster's Market Hall,
And from that vast and noisy place,
The teeming clamour, cry and call.

The Smelly, dirty dust cart now,
Forgotten like the dustbin man,
Who trudged with metal bath aloft,
Cascading hot ash, peel and can.

The dingy fish and chip shop van,
Which parked outside the Sutton Arms,
Long frightened off by safety needs,
And hygiene rules and fire alarms.

And loud explosions sound no more,
'round bonfires which we all had then,
From orange squibs on Guy Fawkes Night,
And bangers bought ten pence for ten,

No mothers calling kids from play,
When having switched the wireless on,
Shouted; "come and have your tea!"
Or "come on quick! Dick Barton's on".

The clatter from the weaving sheds,
The steaming yarn, the carpet flights,
The smoking factory chimney stacks,
The consequential smoggy nights.

The silver spike on coppers hats,
The pulpit where they used to stand,
Directing cars from Vicar Street,
With big white gauntlet covered hands.

And Stubbley's old ramshackle Yard,
Awash with scrap and rusting tins,
Old iron pipes and metal tanks,
And rows of rotting rabbit skins.

We used to walk up to St Mary's,
Ere the planners had their say,
Old Church Street ends abruptly now,
A roaring ring road blocks the way.

The swish and whirr of wire cages,
Shooting out across the room,
The suck and hiss of money tubes,
In Oxford Streets Emporium,

The red carved lion upon the Lion,
And the swan upon The Swan,
The clock tower by the Old Peacock,
So many things like these are gone.

The Central Cinema has gone too,
The last we had of four,
The Empire and the Futurist,
And Grand, are all no more.

Icy slides and workhouse boots,
Ration books and football cards,
Lazy quiet Sunday roads,
Bus conductors, cobbled yards.

These are the lost threads of our life,
Things faded and forgotten now,
Old Kidderminster memories,
So we in turn to change must bow.

The Coming of Trudy and Colin

It was love at first sight when we met Col and Trude',
We would liked to have said but it seemed a bit rude,
To tell them that they were now boarding a wreck,
But they picked up the pub by the scruff of its neck.

And by graft and endeavour, by hook and by crook,
By doing many things that took far more than luck,
With great food and service and selling fine beer,
And by getting it right brought the customers here.

Our Col knows his stuff and the pubs in his blood,
He expresses his pleasure by saying "Very Good",
And Trudy's a Trojan who sometimes looks stern,
'Tho er dow' fool us much we see love and concern.

And even when working and fixing the grub,
They still make some time for the rest of the pub,
To share in the laughter at the things that we say,
Apart from one customer's jokes anyway.

So good luck to them both and long may it last,
Now this place has a future as well as its past,
We drink to your spirit a toast to your dream,
To Trudy and Col and your Wonderful Team.

"Help!"

My Lord I pray you help me,
With my book of rhyme,
I know it's rude that I intrude,
Upon your precious time.

Please know I only do so,
For though I fear to try,
Who will complete this noble feat,
Unless it's you and I.

Through the tiny window,
Which golden time will cost,
If you deny it this last try,
Why then the day is lost.

I feel the metaphors be apt,
To aid you hear my cry,
Unless you act it is a fact,
This bird will never fly.

The lovely eagle will not soar,
Without your flair and stroke,
You are the thing to make it sing,
For I can only croak.

Come my lord the final push,
From you my dear co-founder,
For without this against our wish,
I fear the ship will founder.

Acknowledgments

My thanks to David Lane without whose suggestion, urgings, guidance, edits, corrections, perseverance and patience this could not even have got off the launch pad.

I have also included two excellent poems by Chris Newey ('Toad' and 'The Stationers') and one by Chris Webster. ('Topsy's 65th') which seemed indispensable to this collection drawing as they do from the same well of inspiration.

I would like to thank Murray Vincent for allowing me to use his excellent drawing of the Station Inn.

Cover photography is by Mick Lown. I would also like to thank Linda Fowler of Glint Print for her excellent cover design.

Finally I would like to acknowledge the enthusiasm of my many friends without whose encouragement and generosity I would not have become a raving alcoholic...

Lightning Source UK Ltd.
Milton Keynes UK
UKOW03f2326300514

232626UK00002B/83/P